When?

Mary Elizabeth Salzmann

ABDO
Publishing Company

Published by SandCastle™, an imprint of ABDO Publishing Company, 4940 Viking Drive, Edina, Minnesota 55435.

Printed in the United States.

Photo credits: Adobe, Comstock, PhotoDisc

Library of Congress Cataloging-in-Publication Data

Salzmann, Mary Elizabeth, 1968-
    When? / Mary Elizabeth Salzmann.
      p. cm. -- (Do you wonder?)
    Summary: Simple questions and answers about the times things happen, using the word "when."
     ISBN 1-57765-171-5 (alk. paper) -- ISBN 1-57765-281-9 (set)
      1. Readers (Primary) 2. Readers--Children's questions and answers. [1. Readers.
    2. Questions and answers.] I. Title.

PE1119 .S2348 2000
428.1--dc21

                                            99-046490

The SandCastle concept, content, and reading method have been reviewed and approved by a national advisory board including literacy specialists, librarians, elementary school teachers, early childhood education professionals, and parents.

Let Us Know

After reading the book, SandCastle would like you to tell us your stories about reading. What is your favorite page? Was there something hard that you needed help with? Share the ups and downs of learning to read. We want to hear from you! To get posted on the Abdo Publishing Company Web site, send us email at:

sandcastle@abdopub.com

About SandCastle™

A professional team of educators, reading specialists, and content developers created the SandCastle™ series to support young readers as they develop reading skills and strategies and increase their general knowledge. The SandCastle™ series has four levels that correspond to early literacy development in young children. The levels are provided to help teachers and parents select the appropriate books for young readers.

Emerging Readers
(no flags)

Beginning Readers
(1 flag)

Transitional Readers
(2 flags)

Fluent Readers
(3 flags)

These levels are meant only as a guide. All levels are subject to change.

To see a complete list of SandCastle™ books and other nonfiction titles from ABDO Publishing Company, visit **www.abdopub.com** or contact us at:
4940 Viking Drive, Edina, Minnesota 55435 • 1-800-800-1312 • fax: 1-952-831-1632

I use the word **when** to ask questions about the time something happens.

When do we hug Mom?

We hug Mom **when** she leaves for work.

When do we ride the school bus?

We ride the school bus in the morning.

When do we raise our hands?

We raise our hands **when** we know the answers.

When can I play on the playground?

I can play on the playground during recess.

When do I have my piano lesson?

I have my piano lesson after school.

When do I blow out candles?

I blow out candles on my birthday.

When do I do my homework?

I do my homework in the evening.

When does Dad read to me?

Dad reads to me at bedtime.

Words I Can Read

Nouns

A noun is a person, place, or thing

bedtime (BED-time) p. 21
birthday (BURTH-day) p.17
bus (BUHSS) p. 9
Dad (DAD) p. 21
evening (EEV-ning) p. 19
homework (HOME-wurk)
  p. 19
lesson (LESS-uhn) p. 15
Mom (MOM) p. 7

morning (MOR-ning) p. 9
playground (PLAY-ground)
  p. 13
recess (REE-sess) p. 13
school (SKOOL) p. 15
time (TIME) p. 5
word (WURD) p. 5
work (WURK) p. 7

Plural Nouns

A plural noun is more than one
person, place, or thing

answers (AN-surz) p. 11
candles (KAN-duhlz) p. 17

hands (HANDZ) p. 11
questions (KWESS-chuhnz)
  p. 5

Pronouns

A pronoun is a word that replaces a noun

I (EYE) pp. 5, 13, 15, 17, 19
me (MEE) pp. 21
she (SHEE) p. 7

something (SUHM-thing) p. 5
we (WEE) pp. 7, 9, 11

22

Verbs

A verb is an action or being word

ask (ASK) p. 5
blow (BLOH) p. 17
can (KAN) p. 13
do (DOO) pp. 7, 9, 11, 15, 17, 19
does (DUHZ) p. 21
happens (HAP-uhnz) p. 5
have (HAV) p. 15
hug (HUHG) p. 7

know (NOH) p. 11
leaves (LEEVZ) p. 7
play (PLAY) p. 13
raise (RAYZ) p. 11
read (REED) p. 21
reads (REEDZ) p. 21
ride (RIDE) p. 9
use (YOOZ) p. 5

Adjectives

An adjective describes something

my (MYE) pp. 15, 17, 19
our (OUR) p. 11

piano (pee-AN-oh) p. 15
school (SKOOL) p. 9

Adverbs

An adverb tells how, when, or where something happens

out (OUT) p. 17

when (WEN) pp. 5, 7, 9, 11, 13, 15, 17, 19, 21

23

Glossary

bedtime – the time when you usually go to sleep.

birthday – the day that someone was born.

evening – the time of day between afternoon and night.

homework – work assigned in school that is to be done at home.

lesson – a period of time when a skill or topic is taught.

piano – a large musical instrument with keys that you press to make sounds.

playground – an outdoor area where children can play.